Book Descripti

Does he act mean, rebellic ___ ___. Are
you getting one-word replies back from him? Do you
wish you were closer to him, like old times?

Teenage boys have minds of their own. They also
have mood swings; one day he'll be talkative and
helpful, and the next he'll be gloomy, secretive, and
shallow.

With so many hormonal changes happening inside
them, they are as confused as you are. Parents have it
a little rough, because they've been used to looking
after their boy... and then suddenly, he doesn't need
them anymore. Without proper knowledge on how to
raise this almost-stranger living in your house, who's
been eating like a monster and staying locked in his
room all day, it can be hard to know how to raise
them into being responsible, empathetic, respectful,
and disciplined adults.

In this brief, groundbreaking guide, Frank Dixon
discusses the seven parental skills he finds most
effective in raising, understanding, and
communicating with teenage boys. With his
profound knowledge and expertise in the area, he
offers readers a glimpse into his methodologies in
facilitating parents' raising of confident and
intelligent boys.

Readers will find that his seven vital parenting skills are backed by science, and that they make a remarkable difference in the lives of both parents and teenagers.

With both wit and passion, Frank spills the beans on what works and what doesn't while guiding parents on how to learn each skill, and later apply it to their own boys.

Trust Frank, and you will not regret it!

7 Vital Skills for Parenting Teen Boys and Communicating with Your Teenage Son

Proven Positive Parenting Tips for Raising Teenage Boys and Preparing Your Teenager for Manhood

Frank Dixon

professional advice. The content within this book has been derived from various sources. Please consult a licensed professional before attempting any techniques outlined in this book.

By reading this document, the reader agrees that under no circumstances is the author responsible for any losses, direct or indirect, that are incurred as a result of the use of the information contained within this document, including, but not limited to, errors, omissions, or inaccuracies.

OTHER BOOKS BY FRANK DIXON

**How Parents Can Raise Resilient Children:
Preparing Your Child for the Real Tough World of
Adulthood by Instilling Them With Principles of
Love, Self-Discipline, and Independent Thinking**

❄ ❄ ❄

**How Parents Can Teach Children To Counter
Negative Thoughts: Channelling Your Child's
Negativity, Self-Doubt and Anxiety Into
Resilience, Willpower and Determination**

❄ ❄ ❄

**The Vital Parenting Skills and Happy Children
Box Set: A 5 Full-Length Parenting Book
Compilation for Raising Happy Kids Who Are
Honest, Respectful and Well-Adjusted**

❄ ❄ ❄

**The 7 Vital Parenting Skills and Confident Kids
Box Set: A 7 Full-Length Positive Parenting Book
Compilation for Raising Well-Adjusted Children**

❄ ❄ ❄

**For a complete list, please visit
http://bestparentingbooks.org/books**

YOUR FREE GIFT

Before we begin, I have something special waiting for you. Another action-paced book, free of cost. Think of it as my way of saying thank you to you for purchasing this.

Your gift is a special PDF actionable guide titled, ***"Profoundly Positive Parenting: Learn the Top 10 Skills to Raising Extraordinary Kids!"***

As the title suggests, it's a collection of 10 parenting skills that will help you pave the way towards raising amazing and successful children. It's short enough to read quickly, but meaty enough to offer actionable advice that can make impactful changes to the way you parent.

Intrigued, I knew you would be!

Claim your copy of Profoundly Positive Parenting by clicking on the link below and join my mailing list:

http://bestparentingbooks.org/free-gift/

PROFOUNDLY

POSITIVE PARENTING

Learn the Top 10 Parenting Skills
to Raising Extraordinary Kids!

FRANK DIXON

Before we jump in, I'd like to express my gratitude. I know this mustn't be the first book you came across and yet you still decided to give it a read. There are numerous courses and guides you could have picked instead that promise to make you an ideal and well-rounded parent while raising your children to be the best they can be.

But for some reason, mine stood out from the rest and this makes me the happiest person on the planet right now. If you stick with it, I promise this will be a worthwhile read.

In the pages that follow, you're going to learn the best parenting skills so that your child can grow to become the best version of themselves and in doing so experience a meaningful understanding of what it means to be an effective parent.

Notable Quotes About Parenting

"Children Must Be Taught How To Think, Not What To Think."

— **Margaret Mead**

"It's easier to build strong children than to fix broken men [or women]."

- Frederick Douglass

"Truly great friends are hard to find, difficult to leave, and impossible to forget."

— **George Randolf**

"Nothing in life is to be feared, it is only to be understood. Now is the time to understand more, so that we may fear less."

— **Scientist Marie Curie**

Table of Contents

Introduction

One-word replies, grumbles, grunts, back-talking, lack of discipline, and no respect... wait, is this the diary of a teen boy's parents?

Raising boys is a different ball game, and here's why: unlike girls, boys' mood swings happen rather quickly. One minute they're chilling in the living room, and the next, they're locked in their bedroom. They are inexplicably messier, and they often sleep like logs, eat like the Hulk, and are always in a hurry.

But you're there too, to ensure that they smoothly navigate their way into adulthood. We may not always understand our sons' needs, or what's going in their heads, but that shouldn't stop us from preparing ourselves to understand them better. We must arm ourselves with the right tools to be responsible and admirable parents, so that they follow in our footsteps and not be led astray.

Parents of teenage boys often feel that they don't have the power to steer their child's life in the right direction. The best strategy to combat this is to anticipate the problems before they arise. For starters, we know that as boys reach their teen years, they will go through the many hormonal and bodily changes of puberty. They will be excitable and act a little reckless too at times, but it won't be their fault; their raging hormones compel them to try things they wouldn't otherwise. Thus, parents must keep a vigilant eye on them to ensure they don't get mixed with the wrong crowd, or indulge in self-harming or other dangerous activities.

We have been teenagers once, too; perhaps this is one of the greatest gifts we can offer. We know what it's like to feel so full of energy all the time. We went through the same experiences, and thus, we need to remind them repeatedly that we get it. It is very uncommon for boys to open up with their parents; therefore, we must offer support and a keen ear to lend when they do decide to.

In this guide, we take on the challenge of understanding a teenage boy's mind, and help parents to raise them as confident adults who will enter manhood with improved self-esteem, a disciplined mind, and a self-reliant attitude. We shall look at seven vital parenting techniques and skills that will aid parents in facing the challenges of connecting with their boys.

So, let's dive right in and begin with a basic understanding of what to expect in terms of your boy's cognitive and physical growth as they enter their teen years, and how to brace yourself for the challenges coming ahead.

Chapter 1: Let's Get into the Budding Man's Mind

During adolescence, children continue to grow physically, emotionally, and cognitively. Some of the most prominent and differentiable features in the young boy as they make their way towards adulthood are increases in their size, weight, and height. As they hit puberty, their sexual organs become fully functional, their voices become deeper, and they go through many outbursts of hunger and sleep. Like girls, they also want to become more independent and forge their own identities. But since so much is happening at once, it can be stressful for them—especially if they are early bloomers. When no one in their social circle is going through the same changes, it can make them freak out a little about theirs.

But hitting puberty isn't all bad. It's also the time when teenagers learn about responsibility and power. Although most teenagers are stereotyped for their reckless behavior, like trying new drugs, getting drunk, or engaging in unprotected sex, they still are beginning to make sense of the importance of good friendships, career choices, following their passions, etc. They'll start to think about their future, and whether or not they are doing enough to land a decent college or internship.

We shall discuss this, as well as how parents can help teenagers with their moodiness and surliness, but before we do that, let's discuss the many physical, social and cognitive changes they go through.

Physical Changes Teen Boys Go Through

Puberty in boys doesn't always mark the age of adolescence. Some late bloomers hit puberty well after sixteen, or even eighteen. However, the changes that take place in their mind and especially physicality begin to show up a few years after they've entered the teenage years. You can't be certain when puberty is coming, but some of the most noticeable physical changes include:

- **Body hair:** The appearance of body hair, especially pubic hair, is most commonly among the first signs. Hair will usually grow darker and coarser with time and continue to spread around the thighs, underarms, legs, and chest.
- **Enlargement of Genitals:** As they get older, their genitals (such as the scrotum and testes) will start to grow in size.
- **Increase in Body Size:** Adolescent boys will start to build muscle and gain weight. They may feel clumsy at times, as their legs, hands, and arms will grow faster than the rest of their physique.
- **Swelling of the Chest:** Some teenagers also experience swelling around the nipple region.

This is due to hormonal changes, and is only a temporary condition.

- **Facial Hair:** Facial hair, especially on the chin, neck, and upper lip, will start to grow in length.
- **Oily Skin:** Although breakouts aren't as common in boys as in girls, some still develop open pores. Due to excessive sweating, their skin could also become oily and cause acne to break out.
- **Deeper Voice:** When boys hit puberty, their voices may get deeper. This is also a temporary condition, and they eventually will find their normal range and pitch.

Cognitive Changes Teen Boys Go Through

Did you know that our brains reach their largest size when we are adolescents?

For boys, the brain becomes its biggest at age fourteen; for girls, this happens around the age of eleven. However, this doesn't indicate or confirm in any way that girls are smarter than boys. There are many other changes we can expect to notice in the brain as boys turn into teenagers:

- **Flexibility in the Brain:** Although the brain reaches its biggest size, it still has lots of elasticity for taking in, processing, and storing new information. This also means that it has the potential to adapt, change, and respond to its environment accordingly.

- **Brain Continues to Mature:** Though the brain may stop growing in size after boys turn fourteen, it doesn't mean that it has matured completely. It is still developing, and does so for some eight to ten years from then.
- **The Prefrontal Area Remains Underdeveloped:** The front part of the brain is called the prefrontal cortex, and it takes the longest to mature. In some, it isn't mature until adulthood. This is important to note because this region of the brain is responsible for logical and rational thinking. Its main job is to plan, prioritize, and control impulses. Thus, teenagers often engage in risky behaviors, as they aren't able to assess the depth of their decisions.
- **The Brain Becomes Stressed:** The brain of a teenager becomes more vulnerable to stress than before. This is true for both girls and boys. Pressure from peers, parents, and online influences are all key factors in contributing to the amount of stress teenagers undergo.
- **Developing Mental Illnesses:** The ongoing changes in your boy's body, mind, and emotions can lead to the development of mental health problems. The more stress a teenager feels, the more anxious or depressed they get.

- **Needing More Sleep:** The quantity of melatonin in the body is higher in teenagers, which makes them want to sleep more. It must also be noted that the production of melatonin starts later in the night in most teenagers, which is why they have the habit of staying up late and then sleeping in late. On the whole, you can expect them to require more sleep.

Social Changes Teen Boys Go Through

Emotional or social changes in boys are often a neglected area. Parents assume that all teenagers misbehave, aren't disciplined, or crave more freedom, when in reality, the situation is often a lot more nuanced. Some of the most common social changes you can expect your boy to go through include:

- **A Need to Show Off:** Teenage boys often like to pretend they're tougher than they really are, and be show-offs. They may tell lies and boast about their sexual experiences or their fitness levels.
- **Giving in to Peer Pressure:** Teenage boys are also quick to give in to peer pressure. This can be linked to their need to act cool, so that others don't find them uninteresting. They will go as far as attempting risky behaviors,

like smoking or doing drugs, just because their friends are doing them too.

- **Increase in Aggression and/or Tension:** Increased peer pressure also leads to increased tension and aggression. Boys are more expressive when it comes to exhibiting negative behaviors. They will mostly spend time in their room or hooked to their phones and video games. This can build up tension with others close to them, and also cause mood swings.
- **Need for Independence and/or Power:** Boys will also seek more control over their decisions, from what they wear to what they do in their free time. They may need ground rules about such things, which can sometimes give rise to conflicts.

Teenage Boys and Body Image Issues

Although teen boys aren't as anxious about their appearance as most girls, they still are often dissatisfied with their weight, height, and appearance (Hargreaves & Tiggemann, 2005). When they see their favorite celebrities on TV or follow them on social media, they want to be like them. They want to have the same haircut, the same clothes, tattoos, and even similar hobbies and interests. They internalize societal ideals that they see in TV shows, movies, and sports, and then struggle with low self-esteem.

Men, in general, have always been expected to look ripped, macho, or strong. They have repeatedly been depicted in that manner in pop culture, which informs them that this is what they must look like in order to be desirable. After internalizing these depictions, young boys start to assume that this is what girls like, and then feel dissatisfied and insecure with the way they look. Many boys take up exercise to build body mass, and some even take steroids to improve their physical appearance and sexual performance. According to one study, 38% of teen boys have admitted to using protein supplements to boost muscle mass, and out of those, 6% have admitted to experimenting with dangerous steroids (Eisenberg et al., 2012).

As he moves through puberty and toward adulthood, your teenage boy will begin to observe, and actively partake in, these new changes in his body, mind, and environment. As a parent or guardian, it's important to be cognizant of these changes as well.

Chapter 2: The 7 Vital Parenting Skills to Understanding Teen Boys

Societal constructs often don't let young boys and men express themselves and seek the emotional support they need from their peers, educators, and parents. We have long denied them a listening ear because we think they can deal with their problems on their own. What we fail to see is that they are still too naïve and young to understand the different changes they are going through, and thus need someone to make it all easier.

Thanks to this stoic culture, it has become even harder for parents to approach their teenage son to discuss the various topics they need clarification on. For instance, it is harder to talk to them about drug use, substance abuse, intimacy, and relationships because the gaps between parents and their teenagers have widened. Whenever we do try, sometimes the words fall short, and sometimes we feel too ashamed or embarrassed to keep trying.

But like girls, boys need to be encouraged to open up and be themselves. They need to know that they don't have to conform to the standards that society has set for them, and that they can be as expressive and compassionate as they want to be without being beholden to the "typical man" image in their minds.

What they need is an understanding parent that is willing to share some of the load they carry on their backs, and offer them the support they desperately crave. They want to be understood, heard, validated, looked after, and cared for. Is that too much to ask?

In this chapter, we shall discuss the seven vital parenting skills that will allow parents to be more supportive and present in the lives of their teenage boys. They may look like different creatures with their body hair, increased build, and weird choice of clothing, but they're still your boys! These essential skills will not only help you develop a stronger and meaningful bond with them, but also make room for improved communication and family relations between you and him. The more he feels looked after and supported, the higher the chance that he won't turn to unhealthy or risky behaviors (Neppl et al., 2015).

Let's take a look at these seven skills, now:

Vital Parenting Skill #1: Institute Responsibility

Your son needs to grow up to be responsible. He needs to learn how to own up to his shortcomings, accept his blunders, and make amends. He must be taught to contribute to domestic chores. When parents teach young boys about responsibility, they allow them to taste what power and control feel like, which then prepares them to handle the uncertainties that adulthood brings.

Vital Parenting Skill #2: Provide Structure

Structure and routine make us accountable, too. They allow us to make the most of available hours, with the biggest long-term rewards. Having set expectations and routines can make young adults feel more confident in their capabilities. It also prevents procrastination, and allows your teenager to get things done efficiently.

Vital Parenting Skill #3: Break Stereotypes

Parents must teach their boys about privilege, and to recognize their place in society. They should teach them about the expression of emotions, and encourage them to deal with them in healthy ways. They must be taught to not feel any awkwardness in doing things that the society labels as feminine, and to treat all genders equally and with respect.

Vital Parenting Skill #4: Show Interest

Showing interest in the lives of your teenager allows you to feel more connected with them. It opens doors for healthy and consistent communication to take place, and strengthens the bond between the child and the parent. By showing interest in his activities, passions, and dreams, parents tell their children that they love, value, and care for them.

Vital Parenting Skill #5: Discipline Strategically

Discipline doesn't always mean punishment. It shouldn't involve humiliation and shaming; it has to be more tactical. Teenagers are known to be rebellious, and have a short temper. They are likely to misbehave, or disobey orders when they aren't in the mood for them. This doesn't mean that parents can use verbal or physical abuse to knock some sense into them. Disciplining strategically involves hacks that improve behavior without punishments. It challenges parents to use positive parenting techniques to modify behavior, instead of using abuse or fear.

Vital Parenting Skill #6: Give Privacy

Too much prying into your boy's life can backfire big time. If the goal is to build channels of communication, teenagers must be allowed to have some privacy. Parents who think that prying in their children's lives will make their children open up to them are mistaken. If anything, they will start to hide things and become more secretive than before. They may also start to lie. Thus, we must look at not only the importance of distance and privacy, but also at how parents can maintain a healthy distance from their teenager.

Vital Parenting Skill # Use Restitution

Restitution requires that a person must be held accountable for the mistakes he made and make amends, or face the consequences of his actions. Teaching your child about restitution and how it works will make him more responsible. No one likes to have to face the consequences of their actions. When your boy knows that he will be held accountable for all of his deeds and have to pay for his mistakes, he will be less likely to misbehave.

Let's learn how each of these seven vital parenting skills can be put into practice, and further help us understand our boys and improve communication with them.

Chapter 3: Vital Parenting Skill #1 - Institute Responsibility

In many cultures, men hold the responsibility of arranging the finances for the house. When it comes to house chores, very little is expected of them. Women, on the other hand, have always been portrayed as homemakers. They have to ensure that the kids are fed, dressed, and disciplined. They also have to perform all the domestic duties, like cooking and cleaning.

But, the world is changing. Both partners have to contribute financially, as well as domestically, in the upbringing of a family. Are you doing your part to raise a responsible adult?

You may expect your teenage son to behave like an adult already. But, he is still going through a very beautiful yet confusing transition. His growth is affected, his emotions are becoming stronger, and his anxiety is on the rise too. You may assume that he will figure things out on his own, but believe it or not, he needs your guidance now more than ever.

Teaching responsibility to a budding man is important. You can make them pick up the habit early on by assigning them little chores to carry out. You can praise their contribution to make them feel proud of their effort, and inspire them to be more willing and motivated to contribute further. Responsibility leads to maturity and improved self-worth. It allows the child to feel like they are capable and in control when they do tasks themselves.

Ideally, your boy should now be responsible for looking after his hygiene, homework, room, and cleaning. As soon as he starts to show interest in performing these without supervision or assistance from you, you can decide what more he can assist with in the matters of the house. Sooner or later, he will have to live on his own, which is why you shouldn't feel any shame when asking him for tasks like setting the table, folding the laundry, or doing the dishes.

Why Teach Them about Responsibility?

Parenting is like coaching. We are responsible for coaching our children to do everything. They learn everything from us, such as our eating, sleeping, walking, and talking habits. We shield them against all harm and want to pamper them unconditionally. If it were up to us, we would have never wanted them to grow up! But since they do anyway, they need to know how to manage things for themselves. You can't keep tying their laces for them, or ask them to get in the bathtub every day. You need to teach them to fend for themselves, learn to cook, know basic etiquette, work towards the attainment of their goals, and follow their passions without any fear. In short, they need to be held accountable for the actions and behaviors they exhibit without having to rely on you forever.

Teaching your child about responsibility is crucial for many reasons, one of which being that it promotes a healthy and smart lifestyle. Being responsible requires teenagers to make the most of their valuable time by investing it in activities with long-term benefits. This means they will be occupied with essential tasks, rather than spending all their time watching TV, sleeping all day, or being hooked to their phones. If they know how to cook, they are less likely to indulge in junk food. If they know how to clean, they won't spend their day in a dirty room. If they are aware of the importance of personal hygiene, they will keep themselves clean.

Your boy will also learn about staying away from trouble, or how to get away from it if trouble finds him. Taking responsibility for one's misdeeds is another aspect of learning to own your mistakes and make amends. That also shows how responsible you are as a parent. If you teach him about responsibility, he will feel more capable of taking care of his troubles. You have to take a step back and let him handle things on his own first. If he needs your support or assistance, he will ask for it eventually.

Lastly, in a competitive world like ours, he needs to learn how to take jabs from people. He needs to learn how to take constructive feedback and criticism from others. Teaching your child about responsibility will prepare him to deal with such people and instances without feeling shy or like a failure. It will teach him about resilience, and how he needs to stay in control of his emotions when things don't go the way he planned.

Teaching Responsibility – The How-To

You love your teenager – it's a fact. Your love for him goes beyond expectations. You want to see him happy, but that shouldn't make you want to lose focus on being a parent. Keep in mind that he may be a boy today, but tomorrow, he'll be an adult who has to face the world on his own. He has to form relationships, meet new people, and be expected to be civil and responsible. The question is, are you raising someone like that?

It isn't a secret that parents pamper and shelter their children. The more we do for them, the less they learn about the importance of responsibility. Then, we become the same parents to nag when they aren't unable to keep up with our expectations. But blaming them won't solve the problem. We need to make them see what responsibility looks like, and what happens when they don't become responsible.

Allow Him Choices

He may not feel up for a chore that has been assigned to him. When this happens, parents need to modify their strategy. Offering him choices is a great start.

When you offer choices to your teen, you bind them into having to do at least one of the two chores, while still giving him the freedom to choose. You leave it unto him to decide which one he wants to do.

Include Him in Decision-Making

If you are about to make a decision that concerns him or affects him in some way, let him have a say. If his opinion sounds genuine and sensible, go with it. This is another way to teach your son what responsibility looks like. He chose to put forward that suggestion, and since everyone is going with it, he is now responsible for the outcomes it brings. If things go right, don't forget to praise him. If they don't, let him show accountability and make amends.

Make a List of Chores

When parents choose to pre-plan who does what, it prevents both confusion and procrastination. It also makes one accountable, as they will be held answerable if they fail to do them. To upgrade the list of chores, add in a few positive and negative consequences so that your son is aware of what he gets and loses if he fails to do the chores.

Have Clear Expectations

Clear and concise expectations are also important in preventing misbehavior. If your boy doesn't know what is expected of him, how do you think he will live up to your expectations? Having expectations set and communicated are two different things, with the

nore important. Once your teen knows
ected, it will serve as motivation and drive
work for it. But you have to ensure that the
ations are reasonable and achievable, as
ealistic expectations only lead to frustration and
anxiety.

Set Consequences

Consequences reinforce responsibility. They develop
the connection between a choice and a result. If a
teen makes a certain choice, he has to face the
outcomes too. Having consequences, both negative
and positive, can help teenagers to ponder the
choices they make. It also teaches them to make
sensible choices in the future.

To begin, use the SANE acronym.

- Set small consequences
- Avoid punishing yourself for the poor choices of your teen
- Never abuse your teen with a consequence
- Effective consequences are better when consistent

With these tips, your teenage boy will be acting
responsibly in no time!

Chapter 4: Vital Parenting Skill #2 - Provide Structure

Teenagers can be out of control. They may want more freedom, complain about everything, request more privacy, and demand to have a say in family matters. Freedom always comes with a price. To be able to afford independence, they need to first learn about responsibility and commitment. They need to know what it means to own up to their mistakes, accept their weaknesses, and work on their strengths. They need the vision to follow their dreams, a roadmap entailing the steps along the way, and an undivided focus to strive for the best.

However, all of this requires discipline. Any teenager lacking basic social skills will have a difficult time in his adult life. Discipline and social skills are what make us well-mannered and self-reliant. They make us ready to face the world, as well as the challenges that come with adulthood. To hone their sense of discipline, teenagers need sharp focus and a 100% commitment to stay true to their course without ever losing sight of their goals.

When boys reach adolescence, they start to explore activities that pique their interest. This doesn't necessarily mean that their time is spent on things that matter. For example, your boy may become addicted to video games, which aren't the best use of his spare time. As a parent, your goal should be to teach him how to make sensible choices. This starts with structure.

Why Teenage Boys Need Structure

Routine and structure allow teenagers to be more responsible while teaching them about self-discipline and control. Teens, especially young boys, often struggle with structure in their lives. A good sense of structure can allow them to regulate themselves better for the sake of improvement. Improvement is only possible when one is self-disciplined. Discipline, along with structure, also encourages teenagers to better manage their emotions.

Structure also helps young boys learn about time management. As school gets tougher and expectations increase, teens are likely to be overwhelmed by the many activities that fill their day. Most of the time, they are left with very little time on their hands to spend doing the things they love. Thus, we must teach them how to make the most of their time and spend it on things that enhance their talents and skills rather than on things that add no value. For example, remind them that they only have 24 hours in a day to spend. It encourages them to think rationally and choose between several options. When boys have routines and structure, they can better devote their time to several important activities.

Structure also prevents procrastination, which is another thing many parents worry about. Teenagers are master procrastinators, as they often have no problem delaying things like homework and chores to a later date. Though you shouldn't worry as long as your teen completes his tasks, the thing that you should worry about is their effort.

It is no secret that when we fully commit to something and give ourselves as much time as we need to work on it, our progress and accomplishment show. When we have more time to think, we can get creative and not just do something for the sake of doing it. Teenagers need to be creative, too. They should be encouraged to give their best shot at everything. Having structure in life can help with that.

Having a consistent routine every day can prevent anxiety and depression. We are our most anxious when we feel scared, excited, or short on time. Although many believe that having a complex schedule is what makes one feel anxious, the opposite is true.

Have you ever wondered that whenever we are recommended to start something new like a diet, we are told that we need to bring more structure in our lives? If we see a therapist, they tell us to re-engage in life and start with regular activities to prevent internal anxiety and depression. With expectations running high and peer pressure getting to them, our teenagers are angry, irritated, and depressed. They feel that they need to constantly prove themselves to their parents, peers, mentors, and teachers. To prevent them from going down a dark path, we need to give them a roadmap to success. This is only possible when their days are structured, and they know what milestones to accomplish.

Getting Started with Routines and Structures

If having a structured lifestyle will give our teenagers an edge over the others, it makes sense to create one for them. However, there's no guarantee he will follow it; it highly depends on how the rules are communicated. Teens have a mind of their own. They want to act rebellious and play by their own rules. They will disobey for the sake of disobeying, or to see you get annoyed. But as stated before, if you communicate structure in the right manner, he will soon start doing things out of habit. To help you set the right foot forward, take a look below.

First, identify your routines:

- What routines do you want to begin with?
- What are the important activities you need to map out on paper?
- What should be the order of performing these activities?
- How many times a day should an activity occur, and at what times?

- What is the goal you need to accomplish from setting this routine?

Having answered these questions, you will feel more ready to have a detailed plan laid out in no time. Imagine that the goal is to manage time. How are you going to implement it? Would each task to be done have a designated amount of time? How will you make the most of the available hours? Will each task be repeated every day or between intervals?

Once you have created a chart, or listed the routines, the next step is to explain those routines to your boy. To do so, you have to ensure that he is aware of the end goal you have in mind for him (or that you've decided on, together). He must also know when the goals have to be completed. Remember that because teenagers are so occupied with their lives, they often forget what needs to be done. Thus, set reminders about what they need to do. Place the chart or list in a location where your child can view it easily.

And finally, if they are unwilling to adhere to the set routines and rules, you can motivate them by using positive reinforcement, like setting rewards for completing a task, or praising them for being responsible. You can ask your boy to get on board when deciding how to reward them. That way, he will be more driven to complete the task and follow the routine. If positive reinforcement doesn't work, you may choose to utilize negative consequences instead.

Chapter 5: Vital Parenting Skill #3 - Break Stereotypes

"Toughen up. Men don't cry."

Boys have been told this for years. Even when they are too young to know any better, we tell them to take their traumas "like a man," without even knowing the impact of what we are teaching them. To us, it comes so naturally. We expect our boys to toughen up, even when they are breaking down. We expect them to deal with their problems like grown men, even when they haven't gotten a clue about the next step.

We have, for many decades, given into the cultural stereotyping dictating that men should act tough, and women should be soft. The reason why we as parents need to set the record straight is because this affects the way we interact with our boys, and how they interact with others...as well as how they manage their feelings.

Before we move to break the stereotype, we need to understand what the stereotype is, and why it feels so natural to us. Society has told us that boys have to be strong and confident. They are knights in shining armor, winning wars and women. They have been painted in glory by famous artists, labeled as brave and valiant by poets, and depicted as handsome and charming in the media. This can lead to dehumanization, in that we see them as robots without hearts or an ounce of emotion. And the minute they try to be open and breathe a little, we mock their sensitivity and label it as "femininity."

This also enforces the idea that there are right and wrong feelings. Some feelings are okay for men to have, such as anger and aggression, whereas others like fear, sadness, and grief are too emotional and grounds for silencing. The more we tell them this repeatedly, the more they start to believe in these norms. They start to believe that being loud and pushy is ideal. They start to believe that they have to toughen up, mask their emotions, and act all cool, because the world won't have it any other way. They start to believe that they have to use sarcasm, stoicism, nonchalance, and irritability as their shields. They are then prevented from expressing themselves, or showing their vulnerable side.

This gives rise to a confused generation, where men's feelings and emotions go misunderstood and neglected. When basic needs like the freedom to express joy or grief are silenced, it can lead to several mental health conditions–depression being the most common. In short, boys are expected to appear in control at all times and mustn't appear emotional or weak. As a result, they often hide, downplay, and silence their sadness, fears, and vulnerability.

The Dangers and Damages of Stereotyping

In one study published in the *Child Development* journal, 1,500 children from sixty fifth and sixth grade classrooms across Germany participated in an experiment to show differences in reading levels among genders (Muntoni et al., 2020).. The goal was to provide proof that girls were better at reading than boys, which was a presumed stigma. During the first few sessions, researchers asked the students about how confident they were about their reading abilities, and if they felt motivated to improve their ability to read. The session administered a questionnaire regarding gender stereotyping and reading. After the students filled the questionnaire, their reading ability was tested.

About a year and a half later, the same students were again called in for a session and retested for their skills and reading levels. The boys who had believed in the reading stereotypes earlier showed less improvement than those who didn't believe in it. They also showed less motivation to read, as compared to those who believed that their reading skills and interests (or lack thereof) had nothing to do with the fact that they were boys. The study also reviewed the role of positive peer engagement, and how it benefited the girls in improving their ability to read. For many years, it was believed that boys were supposed to be good at sports and math, and the girls were supposed to be good at reading and art.

The stereotype that boys had weak reading skills created a self-fulfilling prophecy for poor performance and motivation among the boys. The lead researcher, Francesca Muntoni, concluded that stereotypes did affect the mindset of boys, and devalued their actual reading abilities. Less motivation to read resulted in poor performance.

The reason why we need to emphasize the negatives of stereotyping is because it has stopped parents from encouraging children to follow their passion, no matter what that is. We are so accustomed to teaching our boys their assigned gender roles, that it shocks us when they want to break from those roles. For example, in a 2018 analysis reviewing three different studies, it was found that both parents and educators play a crucial role in making their toddler boys act masculine and play with boy toys (Koenig, 2018).

Ditching Labels for Good

Now that we are aware of the dangers of stereotyping and how it can limit one's potential for greatness, we must create an environment for our boys that allows them to be who they want to be. Our only goal should be to encourage and motivate them to go after their passions and dreams, no matter how "feminine" the world defines them. It has to start with us. How do we go about encouraging this?

Accept ALL Emotions

In many homes, cultural stereotypes prevent boys from expressing their emotions healthily. They are told to stop crying because it makes them appear weak, and told to talk loudly because that is how men are "supposed to talk." They are also told to adhere to other socially-acceptable, traditional emotions. But when we raise them in this way, we tell them that it isn't normal to have feelings.

This mindset needs to be discouraged, and boys must be offered every chance to express themselves, especially when they feel their emotions are overpowering them. Don't tell them to wipe their tears in the car when they want to take another ride on the swing because "tears aren't manly." Don't tell them that they shouldn't be sad over their broken heart. Let them be themselves. Let them be humans.

Don't Assign Them Tasks Based on Stereotypes

Just because he is a boy doesn't mean that he will be good with machinery and bad with poetry. Don't assume that he will be better off with sports, and not in drama or arts. When it comes to household responsibilities, we often see men getting assigned certain tasks, such as mowing the lawn or climbing ladders for repairs and installations. We also see women being expected to do the laundry, set the table, or do the dishes. Unintentionally, we have been assigning them tasks based on stereotypes.

Make a conscious effort to avoid this; try creating a list of chores and expecting your teenage boy to pick whatever they like from it. Better yet, have a rotating schedule where he gets to do everything. Additionally, encourage him to do tasks that actively work against stereotypes, such as learning to cook, fold the laundry, and clean the house, because these skills come in handy regardless. Let work be work.

Reinforce Behaviors that Smash Stereotypes

Your teen may not be interested in doing "feminine" chores. He may suspect that if he does them, his peers will make fun of him. To counteract this, place them as a challenge in front of him. For instance, if he is younger, say something like, "I bet you can't fold the laundry or wash the dishes," or "Wearing those colorful socks was a good idea, as they go with your outfit". Or, try normalizing certain behaviors: a father or father figure may say something like, "I cry too sometimes," so your boy knows it's okay to do so himself.

Be Careful of the Words You Use Around Him

The words that we say send out a message about our expectations. When we tell girls that they look pretty, and tell boys how strong they are after they have taken a fall, we are telling them what we expect of their gender. Therefore, from the beginning, use gender-neutral words like "them" instead of "he" or "she". Moreover, when you are using specific terms, don't gender them. For example, instead of saying "fireman," say "firefighter," or "police officer" instead of "policeman."

Encouraging your teenage boy to break stereotypes will help him become a kinder, more socially conscious, and ultimately more empathetic adult–all of which are things that will help him succeed in later life.

Chapter 6: Vital Parenting Skill #4 - Show Interest

Humans are curious beings. As much as we like to inquire about things, we are also interested in the lives of the people around us. For instance, it's natural for a sibling to worry about the other and look after them. It is also natural for your grandma to want to feed you or your children with as much food as she can. It is also natural for educators to worry about the progress of their students. We are social animals, and for a reason. The human race can't survive without interacting with one another. Think about this for a second. How would the world look like if no one interacted with one another? How would it look if no one showed an interest in our lives?

Humans need to interact with, and care about, one another. They need to show interest in the lives of others, especially their partners and children, so that they feel connected and become one another's support system.

When parents exhibit genuine concern and curiosity about their child's dreams, passions, and future, the chances of establishing a strong relationship increases. When children know that their parents support their interests and are keen to know all that is happening in their lives, it makes them feel valued. And as a parent, you don't have to make any extra effort to show affection and interest. You simply have to be present and willing to hear them out when they seek your assistance.

For boys, especially in their teens, this is a rather difficult process. They are less likely to come to you with their complaints and problems than girls are. They would often rather seek assistance and guidance from a peer or mentor instead.

Showing interest in your boy's life will allow you to know them better, and have more things to talk about. The reason it is a vital parenting skill is that it strengthens the bond and allows parents to be more involved in their boy's life.

One of the biggest challenges parents face is choosing what to talk about with their teenagers. Generally, teenagers show interest in various things such as:

- **Controversial Issues:** Questions like, why they can't drive before they are sixteen or can't drink before they are twenty-one.
- **Family-related Issues:** They want to have a say in decisions concerning the family, such as which place to visit during summers, or whether or not the family should move.
- **The Big "Why"s:** Questions about major forces, such as war, racism, spirituality and religion, etc.
- **Personal Interests:** What activities they like, or what passions they have.
- **Their Parents' Marriage:** They might be interested in knowing how you two met, when

you got married, what mistakes you made as a newly-wed couple, etc.

- **Their Future:** They are interested in talking about their prospects, and also concerned at the same time about the uncertainties and weaknesses.
- **Current Events:** They are interested in the world around them and all that is happening in their community, in politics, the economy, and their health (and the health of those around them).

How Showing Interest Improves Communication

The benefits of showing interest in your boy's life are many. When you show interest in his life, he no longer feels alone or left out, and instead feels supported. It helps teenagers in general to unburden themselves and feel a little lighter. It allows them to be more expressive when they see that the person in front of them is interested and curious about what they have to say.

Moreover, when you give your son the chance to be involved, it will also boost his confidence and self-esteem. His teenage years are his years to make mistakes. Your son will make them too. How he copes with failure will determine the level of self-confidence he possesses. If he thinks he can own up to his mistakes on his own, then he is already en route to becoming an emotionally intelligent adult.

But if he isn't, and struggles to deal with the overwhelming negative emotions and resorts to drugs or other forms of substance abuse, they will need someone to prevent them from it and instead turn to healthy ways of coping with them. This person can be you, given the relationship you have with him is strong. When he sees in you a mentor and confidant, it will boost his self-confidence too. He will feel more in control of his emotions, and it will also increase his sense of self-worth.

Finally, one of the scariest things for a parent is secrecy, or lack of transparency. When you don't know what they're up to or involved in, it will only increase your fears and lead to sleepless nights when he is out with his friends. Thus, to encourage honesty and transparency in the house, you need to make communications more effective. He shouldn't only see you as a parent figure but also as a friend. He shouldn't fear coming up to you to inquire about topics that bother him. When you show interest in the things he is interested in, it will give you the leverage to be in the know. You won't have to worry about him lying behind your back, or disobeying rules set by you or your partner.

How to Show You Are Interested in His Life

There are tons of ways you can let your boy see that you are interested in his life, and want to be more included and involved in it. For starters, your general attitude should depict this. Try using affection; being affectionate towards him doesn't mean you have to kiss him on the cheek every night before he goes to bed, but it does mean that you have to make him understand that you're just as invested in his goals and passions as he is. You can start to spend quality time together after school or get started on a fun project together to show him you are interested in his life. Other than that, you can also:

Love What They Love

You aren't as crazy about the musician he loves, or the athletes he admires, or the football team he wants to see play live one day. But you can always make the effort to show happiness and excitement in his excitement. By doing so, you tell him that he is important to you. Keep checks on the celebs, musicians, and other inspirational personalities he looks up to, and stays updated about their lives (and why your boy loves them so much). This will give you ample opportunities to converse. You can even schedule to watch a match together, or go to a concert. You can also show an interest in the company he keeps, or the partner he's dating. That too is a great way to show concern as well as interest in his life.

Ask Concerning Questions

Inquire about his health —emotional, mental, and physical. Go past the generic. For instance, instead of asking about how he's feeling, ask him if anything made him particularly happy, sad, excited, or angry that day.

Ask questions about his school, his friends, or any other relationships he holds close. Show concern over small things, like what they would wear to the school dance or if they have eaten lunch or not. However, there is a fine line between a clingy and a concerned parent. You have to be the latter. You have to probe, but not too much, and the minute he shows irritation, stop.

Spend Some One on One Time Together

Be it on the way home from school, to the park, or simply on the couch in your living room, make time for him even when he doesn't seem interested. Let him see how invested you are. Similarly, when communicating, give him your undivided attention–which means putting your phone down and being all ears. Quality time is one of the greatest gifts we can give to our children and ourselves. After all, these are the memories that we are left with as they move onto the next phase of their lives.

Take Up On A New Project

It doesn't have to be anything as grand as building a treehouse together. You can also get on board with him on a school project, or put a puzzle together. Find things that you two can do together, specifically the ones he is interested in. For example, if he is into sports, you two can spend an evening playing the sport or watching a professional team play one.

Similarly, if he loves to cook, you two can go and take a baking or cooking class together or spend the day baking some goodies together.

Make Eye Contact

Remember we talked about dropping everything and lending him a curious ear? Well, take it up a notch by making eye contact. Eye contact, when made with the speaker, makes a person feel truly heard and seen. This means that you have to listen and notice for any specific awkwardness, fear, signs of depression, or anger in their body movements or facial expressions too. You also have to look him in the eye to let him know that you are giving your undivided attention. Failing to look someone in the eye makes you appear distracted. If you are busy and wish to choose a better time to communicate, let him know subtly.

Chapter 7: Vital Parenting Skill #5 - Discipline Strategically

So he messed up again, didn't he? Isn't this the third time in the week that he has done something stupid? Why does he not learn to do things the right way? The steps are so simple...

Sometimes, our children, especially boys, do things that make us want to deny that we know them altogether. But that is the moment where we need to encourage them to continue trying, instead of discouraging them or dooming them as a failure for life. Just because they did something unpleasant doesn't mean that your love for them has diminished. The right time to support them is when they mess up. Why? Because that is the time when they need it the most to continue moving forward. This is the time when they need someone to come up to them and tell them that they don't need to be ashamed of their mistakes, or feel guilty for trying. This is the time when we need to show compassion instead of denial. We don't need to be paranoid, but rather discipline with kindness and empathy.

But what is discipline? Is it not a synonym of punishment? If you thought so too, you aren't the only parent.

The majority of the parents when asked to discipline their children rely on punishments both simple and severe. With teenagers and their raging hormones, punishments usually come in the form of curfews, being grounded, or having their privileges taken away for a certain time.

But disciplining a teenager or a child, in general, doesn't involve punishments... at least not in its literal sense. The word "discipline" has a Latin origin, and translates to "to teach," whereas the word "punishment" also comes from Latin, and means "to cause pain."

As tempting as it seems to punish them, we never want to hurt or cause pain to our kids. We simply want them to learn from their mistakes. We should make it known to them that our goal isn't to punish, but rather "teach" a lesson so that they know better. The goal should be to discipline, so that they are aware of the natural consequences of their actions and can reflect upon the mistakes they made.

How Discipline Works

Discipline is about shaping behavior. Its goal is to show a teenager how you want them to navigate the world. It involves making your expectations clear, as well as laying out the steps they need to take. It allows them to find motivation and the drive to do the right things, as well as in the right manner, even when no one is watching. For example, they must tell the truth even when you aren't around, or not be tempted to steal when no one is watching. They must also show respect towards elders and be compassionate and kind towards children.

To make it work, sometimes parents need to instate consequences, which not only pose some fear but also serve as motivation. However, when disciplining, ensure that the child knows why they are receiving consequences. They should understand that their actions will eventually impact their life for better or for worse and thus, they should always act responsibly.

Focus on trying to teach a lesson without mocking them for their effort. There has to be a thin line between a concerned talk and a needless, shaming lecture. Punishments make children feel ashamed of themselves, and discourage them. They tell children that they are a failure and are therefore punished for it. However, when we try to discipline them using the right strategies, we are essentially telling them that though we aren't happy with the outcomes, we still want them to try again.

Disciplining Teenagers the Right Way

Since your child has grown beyond the years of time-outs, he will be happiest if sent to his bedroom as a punishment. So how do you make disciplining effective? Let's look at some strategies to help struggling parents come up with ideas that work.

Have Clear Rules

From the beginning, ensure that the rules are set and understood. Teenagers, especially young boys, like to push boundaries to see how their parents will react. If they get some leniency, they try to misuse it. To prevent that, having clear-cut rules and regulations in the house from the get-go is a smart strategy. You don't have to run after them to make them follow the rules, you simply have to address them and discuss the aftermath in a firm yet kind manner. Being kind will portray concern, and your boy will be less likely to disobey as a result. You can also have them design the rules. That way, they will feel included and validated. However, you must have the final say in what works and what doesn't so that they don't get away with too many privileges.

Be Consistent

Making rules isn't the only tool for disciplining. To make them effective, you have to be firm and consistent. Young boys and girls can be master manipulators and negotiators. If given the leverage, they will try to abuse the power and control they have. They are also quick to spot any parental weaknesses. Thus, be consistent about your disciplining strategies. You can't have one parent clean up after their mistakes; you both have to act like a solid team. If you say "no" to them for something and your spouse says "yes," who do you think he will go to the next time he wants something?

Stay Involved

To prevent misbehavior and misunderstanding, always know what your teenager is up to. This doesn't mean you spy on them, put a hidden camera in their room, or browse through their phone for anything fishy when they aren't in the room. This also doesn't mean that you eavesdrop on their conversations or befriend their best friend to know what is going on in their lives. You just need to show interest in their lives and the things that they do. For example, if you are friends with them on Facebook and you notice that they have shared a video about saving polar bears in Antarctica, you can have a grown-up conversation about it during dinner to let them know that you are interested. You can also lend a listening ear if you notice they are going through something, so that they know that the door for communication is always open. You can also plan activities to do together, or trips to go on to during summer break.

Being involved in your teenager's life gives you a heads-up of what they are doing and why. For instance, when you are interested, you may observe signs of distress and depression early on. Then, you can take them to a therapist if they aren't too keen on discussing their issues with you.

Praise

When parents catch their children doing something good and offer praise and appreciation, it makes them more likely to repeat the behavior. For example, if he has abided by the curfew time and home early, let him know that you appreciate it. Make it clear that you noticed this positive action and are happy about their decision. This tactic makes the reinforcement of the said behavior more likely to occur again, and also makes your teen feel valued and cared for.

Give Natural Consequences

Knowing the consequences of his actions can make your teen feel more responsible. For example, you can tell him that if he doesn't study, he won't pass with a good grade. Or, if he doesn't learn to drive responsibly, he won't be given a car of his own. Consequences, when tied to the choices he makes, can make your teen accountable for them.

Let Them Face the Consequences

If they still don't listen, or mock your rules and concerns, let them face the consequences of their actions. Natural consequences are sometimes the best teacher. Some stubborn kids learn things this way.

We ͷave all come across the term "man cave." Although your boy is still not an adult yet, he needs his space and privacy more than ever now. He is going through many physical changes that he can't even talk to you about, or discuss with his peers openly. He is also dealing with a set of emotions he never felt too strongly such as jealousy, love, envy, anger, or anxiety. Unlike girls, he doesn't want to talk about things in detail or share his experiences. He needs to figure it out himself. Thus, the need for privacy.

Although we are socially-bound to crave interactions, sometimes we want to allow a certain amount of access to the people around us. Teens want the same. They want to be able to have the right to decide how much access someone has to their personal lives. According to Alan F. Westin, a professor Emeritus of Public Law and Government and a best-selling author, privacy is a claim made by an individual, a group of them, or by an institution to determine for themselves to what extent they want the information about them to be shared or communicated to others. This also applies to countries or sects that wish to stay remote and inaccessible to the main public. Think North Korea, or many rural tribes in South Africa.

We all have traits that compel us to widen our circles, soak in new information, and meet new people. Sometimes, a little peace of mind in the form of isolation isn't unheard of. This desire for privacy in teenagers is natural and critical, as it pushes them to develop an unobstructed zone for themselves. They feel safe in that space; they feel they aren't being judged or criticized, and can hear their thoughts and vent out their feelings without having to conform to established rules made by society.

Why Do Young Boys Need Privacy?

What does privacy mean to a teenager? Does it only mean that he will have his room locked the minute he comes home? Does it only mean that he will avoid taking calls in front of you, or spending time with you doing things together?

Privacy is more than that. It is an expression of independence and freedom. He doesn't want his parents or siblings sitting on his neck 24/7. He doesn't want them to be concerned about him like before. He doesn't want to have to tell his parents where he is, what he is doing, or who he is with. He wants to be able to have a friend over and not have parents roam around the hallways being inquisitive. He needs space where he can think independently, and not be bombarded or invaded by others. Privacy has more to do with eliminating the mental clutter in the head than in the room. Your son needs privacy and control to make decisions for himself. He wants to be able to wear what he wants, befriend whoever he wants, and do things in his style whenever he feels like. He doesn't need others dictating things to him.

This, to him, is the meaning of privacy.

How to Respect Their Need for Privacy

It can be hard to balance your desire to know what your son is up to with the need to not be too prying. Your reasons to keep a check on his activities are natural; after all, you have been doing so from the time he was born. However, he doesn't need you as often now as he did before, and that can be depressing.

So, how do you respect his need for privacy without losing your control and give him what he needs within set parameters? Let's take a look:

Don't Be Nosy

This is a given. You can't be nosy. Don't dig too much into his things or sneak into his room to look for something suspicious. Never eavesdrop onto his conversations, because that is a breach of trust. Furthermore, don't try to dictate who he should or shouldn't be friends with. This will annoy him, and in a deliberate attempt to get back at you, he might engage in bad company that can hurt him in the long run. Being nosy or too inquisitive is never acceptable because it takes away a child's liberty and freedom. When you pry on him, you are essentially saying that he isn't smart enough on his own, or that he can't make sensible decisions. This can drive him away from you, which is the exact opposite of what you have been trying to do.

If you still can't control yourself to not be inquisitive, imagine how would you feel if someone did the same to you? Would you not feel judged and manipulated? Would you not feel trapped or imprisoned?

Your first step is to do your best not to be a nosy parent. Do not go digging around your teenager's belongings. Never try to listen in on conversations. And avoid trying to keep your kids away from friends or activities out of spite to try to keep them safe.

Don't Investigate – Probe Instead

Not all teenagers are talkative. They like to keep some things private. Probing is good, because it allows you to play it safe. It involves piquing his interest, but not too much. You want him to come to you. So you deliberately, but subtly, ask questions about things that concern you but stop the minute you sense that he is getting irritated or bothered. This technique of communication will allow you to give back the power to him and establish a good rapport with him in return. Asking, not demanding, is key.

Keep Your Hands Bound

Intruding isn't allowed either. If you keep looking for moments to sneak into their bedroom to look for some clue or to find something dangerous every time he leaves his room, you are being paranoid. Unless you are certain that there is some problem you need to take care of, like why are his grades falling or why does he seem sleepy all day, you have no business in sneaking into his room or checking his drawers or personal laptop. Also, make it a habit to knock before entering his room, as it shows that you respect his privacy and space and don't want to invade it unnecessarily.

Don't Try to Befriend His Friends

You may want to try to act like the cool parent and hang out with his buddies from school or neighborhood, or want to stay in the room with them when they all are hanging out, but don't. Even if you are close to your teenage son, you don't fit in. No matter how friendly you guys are at home, when he is with his friends, he is a completely different individual. It's okay to walk in on them a few times when they are in your house, but don't make it a habit to hang around for too long. His friends might not mind, but he might. Would you prefer that they hang out at some other place, instead? Therefore, don't give him any reason to want to choose another place or time.

Chapter 9: Vital Parenting Skill #7 - Introduce the Rule of Restitution

Do you ever feel that your son got away with less punishment than he should have gotten? Maybe not punishment in the literal sense, but you feel like you could have chosen a better way to instill discipline than by just taking away his phone for the weekend? Think about it: do things like these make a difference in his behavior? Does he give up the behavior that got him into trouble the first time? Or does he repeat it a week or month later?

If you feel the same way, then you aren't the only parent in this boat. Sometimes, we need to make consequences a little scarier or memorable to prevent negative behavior, as well as instill some discipline in our kids.

This is where restitution comes in. By definition, restitution is the method where we allow our children to face the consequences of their actions without intervention or any leniency from anyone, including parents. This means that if they don't study for their exams, they fail their tests. It means that if they are too lazy to wake up in the morning on time, they miss the school trip they had been looking forward to for weeks. It sounds harsh, but restitution is the best way to teach children how to respect others and exhibit well-mannered behavior.

The restitution method is one of the most effective disciplining strategies in classrooms. Often referred to as restorative justice, it holds children accountable for their misbehavior. If your son misbehaves, let him be schooled by a stranger for having poor manners instead of covering up for him. Also, make him apologize for being rude and disrespectful.

Putting Restitution to Practice

Have you tried using external rewards to encourage good behavior and discipline? Did you feel that every time you rewarded your teen for something good, they demanded more, and soon, you were taking in requests as if collecting tickets to the roller coaster ride?

And have you experimented with punishments too, only to end every argument with yelling, anger, or the door being slammed in your face? Even if our anger or rewards get our kids to behave for the time being, does it promise anything in the future? The most important question of all is whether or not we are facilitating our boys to become independent, self-disciplined, motivated, and responsible problem-solvers. If not, then what are we doing?

The reason restitution is different and an essential parenting tip is because it doesn't focus on rewards or punishments, but rather on understanding the depth of the actions. It focuses on the "why" of things, such as why do kids misbehave, what are their triggers, why they act angry and annoyed when asked a simple question, etc. Restitution allows teenagers to face the consequences of their actions in a logical way, where they understand that their actions cause certain outcomes.

Restitution gives your teenager a chance to make amends as well as make compromises. For example, if he punched a hole in the wall out of anger, he must pay for the patchwork from his lunch money or weekly pocket money. If he deliberately acts out and abuses someone verbally, he must earn their respect once again by doing whatever it takes after he has apologized. It may seem that restitution has more to do with shame and humiliation, but it isn't. No parent would ever want to shame their child. The purpose is simply to make him accountable for his actions, own up to them, and make amends wherever necessary.

How to Get Started with Restitution

The rules to put restitution into practice are varied. It doesn't involve making your child stand out in the yard holding a sign that says, "I was wrong." We have to differentiate between punishment and discipline. We need to use strategies that help improve behavior, not just eliminate bad behavior for the time being. Here's how you can get started with restitution techniques.

Let It Make Sense

Restitution has to make sense. You have to be strict about making them face the consequences, and not cover for them. If they have gotten themselves into trouble, they have to come up with ways to crawl out of it. Additionally, negative consequences should be directly linked to negative behavior.

Let Them Have a Say

Having a say in determining what the restitution should be for misbehavior is also a good start. Both you and your son should mutually decide on the consequences, and under what conditions they apply. When your child feels included this way, he will be less likely to disappoint you as you allowed him to engage. This shows a friendly exchange where he knows that he shouldn't make mistakes or hurt anyone, and what will happen if he does. Even if he commits fault, he will at least have the guts to acknowledge and accept it.

Walk the Talk

They look up to you for things. They learn behaviors from you, take up after your actions, and consider you a role model. However, if you aren't being the right role model, you are the reason for their lack of social skills and disobedience. They need to see you owning up to your mistakes, so that they feel no shame in doing it too. They need to see you making amends so that they become responsible for their actions too. Model what you preach.

Set Up Other Consequences

If the misbehavior and disobedience continue after they have made amends, it is acceptable for you to combine restitution with other consequences, too. Sometimes, restitution fails to model the correct behavior, and thus, we need to remind the child what more could happen to them if they continue to misbehave.

Conclusion

Believe it or not, raising a well-mannered, decent, and compassionate teenager isn't hard. It's just that parents have heard so much about how difficult it is, they always feel a little under-prepped. This brief guide provides you with the right tools and strategies you need to get started. The secret is to start early; train him from an early age so that when he grows up, he doesn't feel entitled or privileged to certain perks. Additionally, being a little strict, consistent, and firm about the rules and regulations is also another great strategy to put to practice.

When parents are consistent and firm about their rules, there are fewer chances of misbehavior and arrogance from the teen's end, which are the two most common challenges parents face. Another important thing, as previously discussed, is breaking the stereotypes. We need to remind him that they are no greater than the opposite gender. We need to tell them that they both should be treated equally. You tell them that doing chores that the world classifies as "feminine" isn't a real thing, and that young boys shouldn't feel any shame in doing them.

We must make them responsible, kind, and compassionate. We must prepare them for the next phase of manhood, as such social skills are highly valued in the professional world. We must teach them about the importance of routines and rules, and why they must adhere to them.

If you recall, we also discussed why we need to use restitution. They need to know how to own up to their mistakes, accept them, and face the consequences of their actions.

Finally, teach discipline strategically. Boys tend to misbehave, and punishments only make them more obstinate. Thus, you have to discipline them in a strategic manner where they don't feel that they are being lectured or punished over something, but rather view it as an improvement strategy.

When raising young boys, make an effort to understand them, try to make communications more effective and deep, learn to respect their privacy, and don't pry too much. You want to raise them to be confident and mature adults, and that is only possible if they feel respected and self-reliant. They need to feel freedom. They need to experience what independence looks like.

Hopefully, this will be all that you need to raise a resilient, emotionally-intelligent, and compassionate young boy.

Thank you for giving this book a read. I hope you loved reading it as much as I enjoyed writing it. It would make me the happiest person on earth if you would take a moment to leave an honest review. All you have to do is visit the site where you purchased this book: It's that simple! The review doesn't have to be a full-fledged paragraph; a few words will do.

Your few words will help others decide if this is what they should be reading as well. Thank you in advance, and best of luck with your parenting adventures. Every moment is a joyous one with a child.

References

Bare, L. (2019, March 7). Why Do Teenage Boys
Need Structure? Psychology Today.
https://www.psychologytoday.com/us/blog/
boys-will-be-boys/201903/why-do-teenage-
boys-need-
structure#:~:text=Teenagers%2C%20especia
lly%20teenage%20boys%2C%20need

Chakravarty, C. (2014, December 19). 10 Handy Tips
On How To Make Your Teenager
Responsible. MomJunction.
https://www.momjunction.com/articles/han
dy-tips-make-teenager-
responsible_00118480/

Eisenberg, M. E., Wall, M., & Neumark-Sztainer, D.
(2012). Muscle-enhancing Behaviors Among
Adolescent Girls and Boys. PEDIATRICS,
130(6), 1019–1026.
https://doi.org/10.1542/peds.2012-0095

Ginsburg, K., & Pontz, E. (2019, March 18). Having
trouble disciplining your teen? This expert
explains why. Parent Toolkit.
https://web.archive.org/
web/20200202003042/http://
www.parenttoolkit.com:80/general/news/
general-parenting/rethinking-discipline-for-
teens

Hargreaves, D. A., & Tiggemann, M. (2005). Idealized media images and adolescent body image: "comparing" boys and girls. Body Image, 1(4), 351–361. https://doi.org/10.1016/j.bodyim.2004.10.002

Koenig, A. M. (2018). Comparing Prescriptive and Descriptive Gender Stereotypes About Children, Adults, and the Elderly. Frontiers in Psychology, 9. https://doi.org/10.3389/fpsyg.2018.01086

Lee, K. (2019, July 4). Most Effective Ways to Discipline a 6-Year-Old Child. Verywell Family. https://www.verywellfamily.com/discipline-strategies-for-school-age-kids-620099

Linetti, L. (2019, March 29). Why Is It Important To Teach Your Child Responsibility - Thrive Global. Thriveglobal.Com. https://thriveglobal.com/stories/why-is-it-important-to-teach-your-child-responsibility/

Morin, A. (2019, February 20). These Consequences Will Change Your Teen's Behavior. Verywell Family. https://www.verywellfamily.com/discipline-strategies-for-teens-1094840

Muntoni, F., Wagner, J., & Retelsdorf, J. (2020). Beware of Stereotypes: Are Classmates' Stereotypes Associated With Students' Reading Outcomes? Child Development. https://doi.org/10.1111/cdev.13359

Neppl, T. K., Dhalewadikar, J., & Lohman, B. J. (2015). Harsh Parenting, Deviant Peers, Adolescent Risky Behavior: Understanding the Meditational Effect of Attitudes and Intentions. Journal of Research on Adolescence, 26(3), 538–551. https://doi.org/10.1111/jora.12212

NIMH » The Teen Brain: 7 Things to Know. (n.d.). National Institute of Mental Health. https://www.nimh.nih.gov/health/publicatio ns/the-teen-brain-7-things-to-know/index.shtml

Puberty: Adolescent Male. (n.d.). John Hopkins Medicine. https://www.hopkinsmedicine.org/health/we llness-and-prevention/puberty-adolescent-male

Quick Tips | Creating Structure | Essentials | Parenting Information | CDC. (2019, November 5). Centers for Disease Control and Prevention. https://www.cdc.gov/parents/essentials/stru cture/quicktips.html

Wilson, J. (2018, April 22). Your Roadmap + 10 Tips: How To Raise A Boy Right (and Keep Your Teen Boy Emotionally Healthy). Parent Remix. https://www.parentremix.com/blog/2018/4/22/how-to-raise-a-boy-right

Printed in Great Britain
by Amazon